Lake District Stone Walls

By the same author:
West Country Stone Walls (Redcliffe Press, 1979).

Lake District Stone Walls

**Looking at random walls in Cumbria
by Janet Bodman**

Janet Bodman 30.4.84

**Dalesman Books
1984**

The Dalesman Publishing Company Ltd.,
Clapham, Via Lancaster, LA2 8EB.
First published 1984
© Janet Bodman 1984

ISBN: 0 85206 777 1

With gratitude for Frank's steadfast encouragement.

Printed in Great Britain by Fretwell & Brian Ltd.,
Healey Works, Goulbourne Street, Keighley, West Yorkshire.

CONTENTS

Cover photographs:- Front: Bridge End, Little Langdale (Bob Matthews). Back: Hawkshead (Michael Turner).

Illustrations 6, 7, 10, 12, 14 and 15 converted into monochrome from colour slides by Bob Bowen LRPS.
Diagrams by permission of the British Standards Institution.
Fig. 2 reproduced from 'Geology and Scenery' by permission of the Lake District National Park.

1. **Lake District stone walls — as seen in the farmhouse, barn, outbuildings, bridge and field boundaries at Watendlath.** *(F. Leonard Jackson)*

PREFACE

WHEN in the Lake District you are always aware of the grand stone environment in the landscape and the buildings. Here are some of the oldest, hardest rocks in England. There is granite and slate as in Cornwall, but the Cumbrian varieties have some wonderful colour ranges, and together with other stones provide the region's remarkable building materials. The great drystone boundary walls climbing over the fells are immediately eye-catching. They have been well described in William Rollinson's *Lakeland Walls,* and so will be considered here quite briefly.

Our study is of houses, farms, barns, bridges and many garden walls which are built in what is known in the trade as 'random' style, and all these are mortared. Among the variety is one particular method of construction known as 'watershot' or 'weathershot' which is unique to the Lake district. All random work is of hard, rough, little-cut stone, in contrast to finely worked, softer, 'ashlared' stone used for more formal constructions. So random walls are found on the traditional, modest domestic buildings. The men who build these robust, frequently beautiful constructions are usually highly skilled craftsmen, and are often from families with long traditions of working with stone. Teaching has been passed from father to son for generations and these same training traditions may still be found in just a few quarries.

The hope here is that you will look more closely at random walls as you pass, and will use every chance of talking with the stone workers wherever they can still be found. Each mason, waller or quarryman I have been privileged to meet has talked with enthusiasm of his work. They naturally use the local names for their tools, and the processes of sorting, hammering and splitting or laying stones. Pride in their craft shines through, and they will gladly share their knowledge. Long may this continue as it is a craft which deserves the fullest possible recognition.

This can only be a brief survey: it is not a definitive study of all the geological features or all the Cumbrian quarries, but it covers each of the building stones in their particular areas, and suggests some sightings in the hope that the exploring reader will discover many more.

Acknowledgements: I wish to express my indebtedness to all those who have helped in this study, particularly Albert Bowness and his son Richard, and all the other stoneworkers; also Martin Bodman, Margot Dickson and Arch Ireson for their editorial advice; and Mary Burkett and Eva Chew for their support.

7

HISTORY

THE Lake District is an area where, apart from slate, the stone is not easy to work. The region was somewhat isolated from the rest of the country until this century due to its mountainous barriers. Early influences on domestic buildings are not easy to define as the prehistoric and medieval houses are hard to distinguish in archaeological finds. However there is evidence of some early settlements, and there are stone circles as standing reminders of the settlers.

The time between the prehistoric and medieval period belongs outstandingly to the Romans. They were the first notable invaders, but they were military outsiders who occupied their own forts and camps. Their famous legacy was of course Hadrian's Wall. In spite of the four hundred years of their occupation there is not much evidence of Roman influence on subsequent building styles in the region. Hadrian's Wall was built with well-cut squared stones, brought to regular courses with engineer's precision driving it over the hilly terrain. The only sign of random style is the occasional small stone wedged into crevices here and there.

After they had gone, leaving their hybrid civilisation when Rome fell, the perennial settlers moved in, up the river valleys. First came the Saxons, followed by Danes, then Norsemen from the Isle of Man and Ireland. As in Yorkshire, the Danes tended to stay in the lower valleys, and the Norsemen with cattle and sheep scattered for preference over wide areas in the fells and heads of valleys. (Place names on the map show this distribution by Norse 'Thwaite' and Danish 'Thorpe' for instance.) Later the Scots came, and the border with Scotland was not finally settled in this stormy corner, termed the Debatable Land, until the mid-sixteenth century.

As in several other mountainous countries in Europe and beyond, the sheep and cattle were traditionally taken up to some of the high fells during the summer for the valuable high pasturage. Small stone buildings were used seasonally like the Scots' shieling, or the Norwegian saeter. Now only the eighteenth century field or bank barns can be seen in the 'outfields', some way from the farms. Their walls are often random, and the early field enclosures running out from the valley farms are still in evidence.

In the eighteenth century 'the pace of the new phase of enclosure was quickened through the division of open land by agreement, and by Act of Parliament. During this period the tall drystone walls which march up the fells, dividing the slopes into large square fields, were erected in a concentrated endeavour which is still the wonder of visitors from the South . . . these may represent the walling technique at its best.' (Brunskill's *Vernacular Architecture of the Lake Counties*). These boundary walls are entirely drystone, without mortar, and vary in the type of stone used, but a

8

random effect is produced by the mixture: sometimes thin angular slate-stone is combined with split rounded cobblestones.

The houses of the region were to meet men's needs during its changing history. First the large fortified stone houses with their pele towers, for look-out and defence purposes, were built with walls four feet thick, usually of random style. People and cattle would be hurried inside at the time of the many border raids. Bastle houses, with means of passive defence, were smaller and without towers. Farmhouses were built in the long-house tradition, that is a long building with living accommodation for humans at one end and animals at the other. This ancient tradition was to be found also in Devon, Cornwall, Northumberland, Scotland, Wales, Ireland and Scandinavia.

Many of the long farms seen today were probably built on the site of the earlier long-houses. It is interesting to note how many of them now show a marked distinction between the domestic buildings and the animals' quarters. This is achieved in different ways: the house walls may be whitewashed random stone to upgrade it from the bare stone farm buildings, or the house may have dressed stone in contrast to the whitewashed barns and outbuildings.

Small stone houses for the yeoman or tenant farmer were put up in the seventeenth century, and later in the eighteenth century cottages were built for workers such as weavers and bobbin-makers. Then with the Industrial Revolution came the larger water-powered mills, and new industries where the local tradition continued in the face of new problems in constructing furnaces and chimneys. Finally ugly structures, precisely designed, took over the skyline in Barrow and Millom for instance.

In the rural scene the thread of history has remained constant to the present day; it is the seventeenth and eighteenth century farms and cottages that we still admire, and they have remained the model for good basic building standards.

BUILDING STONE : COLOURS AND SOURCES

THIS is a region with a fine variety of stone building materials. The rocks are amongst the oldest in Europe, and the visitor is immediately impressed by finding the majority of buildings are of stone. In *Portrait of the Lakes* Norman Nicholson observes 'the stone wall is the basic unit of Lake architecture. Cottages, farms, manor-houses and even villages are stone walls set together at angles and roofed over in parts.' And of course, as in all other stone regions, most of the buildings reflect the underlying geology. It is complex, but a simplified pattern can be seen in the three distinctive areas which run parallel, on south-west and north-east lines.

Skiddaw rock and slates.   These oldest stones, of the Ordovician era, are sedimentary, and create the foundations of the most northerly of the three areas. Keswick stands at the southern boundary.

Borrowdale volcanic series (B.V.S.).   Here the volcanic lava and ash were thrown up through the old rock, then hardened and pressurised in various ways. Here you find the Lakeland Greenstone, very different from the Skiddaw slate. This is in the heart of the whole region and is in the central area of the three. Ambleside is on its southern boundary.

Silurian rocks.   These are sedimentary grits, shales and flagstones, which created the characteristic foothills, in contrast to the mountains to the north. In this third division Kendal lies on its southern edge.

   Like separated jig-saw pieces, in outer rings beyond the three large areas, are:

Mountain (carboniferous) limestone — lies south and north-east.

New red sandstone — in the west coast and north, and north-east of the region.

Granites — in outcrops curving from Eskdale and Threlkeld to Shap.

Cobbestone — found in many places throughout the region.

Skiddaw rock and slate

   This oldest stone occurs over a large area; a sedimentary sillstone hardened, and later thrust up to form the northern mountains. The slate is not good building stone, and looks jagged and fragmented in rough boundary walls. The rock however can be used for building, and Keswick shows this dark grey on the majority of its houses and shops. Yet there is a good dark brown variation which gives relief to the eye. And there are still brighter results when a few imaginative mixtures have been tried out. Coming into the town from the south, and after dropping down the hill, a terrace on the right shows up as grey stone, and some touches of red sandstone have been added to the blackish Skiddaw stone. And when leaving for

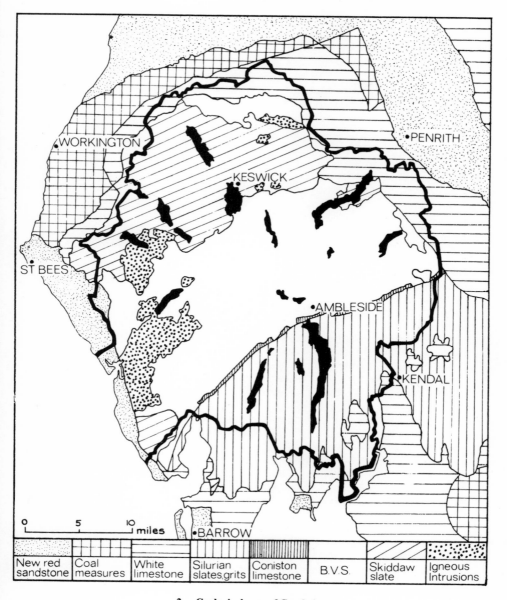

New red sandstone	Coal measures	White limestone	Silurian slates, grits	Coniston limestone	B.V.S.	Skiddaw slate	Igneous Intrusions

2. Geological map of Cumbria.

the south again on the A591, up on the right curve of the hill, there is an interesting mix of colours on the walls of a modern house.

At Threlkeld, a little to the east, some rather fine rich brown walls can be found, which probably have an iron oxide component to produce such a black treacle shade, within their peat-like blocks. The old houses in this village, as in so many others, show their sturdy traditional proportions of native good sense — the buildings are truly indigenous.

Slate of the Borrowdale volcanic series (B.V.S.)

This is proably the most remembered stone for outstanding colour in the region. It is found on roofing tiles of course, but nowadays more frequently in house cladding and walling and National Park signs, house names and monumental work. The colours can be dark grey and brownish grey, but most remarkable and unique are the green slates. There is a dark green from Honister, a quarry worked for three hundred years, and the lighter grey-green of Kirkstone, while Coniston gives two green shades, with variations in several quarries such as Broughton Moor or Moss Rigg and others. Local names are evocative, 'light sea green' or 'olive green'. The shades are hard to define in one title, as their varying conifer greens change in differing lights, times or shadows of trees and deep valleys. They liven up in the sunlight and gleam in the rain.

If you have no time to explore the quarries and want to see labelled specimens easily, the display in the Tourist Information Offices at Keswick and Ambleside and the Brockhole Centre are excellent. But as they are indoors and dry these are less exciting than in their own context.

Some of the older green slate farm buildings and houses are found in the heart of Borrowdale, in Grange. And Hawkshead provides examples in some new house walls, and green porches of council houses. Walls are usually made from off-cuts of random greenstone slate, after the finest has been selected for polishing to marble-like perfection. There are showrooms at Skelwith Bridge, with produce from Kirkstone, or there are workshop/studios to be found like one in north Keswick where the stone can be seen close at hand, and possibly being worked. The green slate is so much appreciated that you will find it in many places in London, such as the Times building and St Thomas's Hospital; and even as far afield as the Berlin Zoo and in America, Canada and Australia.

Ambleside itself is built of various stones; some are green, but a number of Victorian houses are of the stone of its southern neighbour — the dark sombre Silurian. If mixed with lighter grey or green or brown the effect is more cheerful. The Public Library in Ambleside has a pleasant light grey random Lakestone which demonstrates the interesting 'watershot' technique.

Finally there are also the less frequent, unforgettably beautiful blue-grey slates from this area, and some further south from Brathay quarry. One of the finest displays can be seen on the roof of the Chelsea Pensioners' Hospital in London. Above those cheerful pink brick walls these tiles are

3. **Dark Silurian stone mixed with lighter stones as seen at Ambleside old church.** *(W. R. Mitchell)*

shown to perfection. It is interesting to find that Sir Christopher Wren ordered them from Buttermere — west of Honister.

Silurian Stone

This is found extensively in the third and most southerly area. It is hard, durable and good for building, but most of it is a gloomy grey-black due to grey shale embedded in the old grits and flagstones. Houses, farms, cottages and roadside walls are built of this right through from Kendal to Ambleside. In the small towns bordering Windermere, many large and pretentious nineteenth century private and public buildings can look over-powering with their mourning shades, with unnecessary embellishments. In dark weather they are grim. Yet the dry walls, farms and bank barns, with ramp entrances, up in the fells appear to fit into their surroundings; even more so when they have collected lichens and ferns.

Some of the stones show various browns, sand, tan and rust, and these together with the dark grey are more lively than walls of unrelieved charcoal. In several villages the mixture is noticeable, and examples appear in Hawkshead in some old houses and the church, which is no longer white plastered, so showing its random style.

Not surprisingly Kendal appears to have fewer buildings of its own Silurian stone and many more of the neighbouring white limestone, which runs up from the south-west. There is some new random work to be seen on several end walls of the Longlands School buildings, north-east of the town on the Appleby road. The stone is 'imported'. Greenstone for some, and a buff limestone for others, have been used. Each in its way is a decorative and eye-catching advocate for random walling.

Mountain (carbiniferous) limestone

In the south of the Lakes the stone is related to the Pennine limestone. Several writers praise its brilliance, and in *Portrait of the Lakes* Norman Nicholson claims it as 'one of the loveliest rocks to be found in the whole district . . . and the stone walls, the cottages, the farms look as if they had been scrubbed . . . In Furness you are never allowed to forget you are in limestone country because of the whiteness of the buildings.'

There can hardly be a greater contrast to the neighbouring area's heavy grey Silurian stone, and the southern approaches to Kendal will give sightings of recently built walls beside the feeder roads and the A65. There are retaining walls, bridge piers and boundary walls, some of which run like an ornamental crest topping the high cuttings, and raw outcrops of limestone show up on the embankments. In Kendal itself there are many buldings of this stone, taken from Kendal Fell in the last century. The nearby village of Burneside displays some good random walls in Hall Park council estate. The manager of the Cumbria Stone Quarry recommended this as worth a visit, with justifiable pride, which one hopes the builder shares. (The limestone can be seen in detail in the Crosby Ravensworth showrooms of this quarry.)

A red variation, stained with haematite ore, lies in the north-west, in the

Cockermouth area, but the most interesting variety is in the unusual pink limestone found in the north. A few shop fronts of this colour show up in Penrith. However the purest example, and the most elegant, is Dalemain Hall. The stone is a pale mushroom pink; seen across the green park from the road it is unforgettable. Nearby is Dacre where both the church and castle have some of the pink, but it is mixed with a buff shade in the castle and pink shading to lavender and claret in the church. The east end of the south aisle displays this well. There is red sandstone here too, in the older east end, and on door and window facings.

The buff limestone comes from Orton Scar quarry. Examples will be seen in some splendid old barns, standing close to the A6 on the right, within a few miles of the southern approach to Penrith. The large quoins, or corner stones, vary in colour and the builders have made a lively pattern by mixing red sandstone and other darker stones with the light fawns and tans, only broken by the long ventilation slits. From Orton Scar quarry also comes a very beautiful fish grey limestone which can be polished. This is strikingly displayed, with all its embedded fossils, on the entrance floor of Kendal's Abbot Hall Art Gallery and in the churches at Appleby and Dent.

New red sandstone

This is found in the cliffs and buildings of St Bees, and in many other places all along the south-west coastline, including Barrow. It reappears in the north-east in the Eden valley, and from there in a line to join the sea again north of the Workington region of coal measures. Penrith and Carlisle have many buildings from this source, and good examples can be seen in Beckermet near Winscale. It is a warm cheerful dark terracotta, but I find it lacks sparkle and so has a dark and weighty appearance which together with erosion can be depressing, as seen in Penrith Castle. When however, it is used for facings this can be as effective and fine as brick of the same colour.

Granite

This is an ancient crystalline rock of volcanic origin and contains mica, quartz and feldspar. The proportions of these vary tremendously, and so do the effects. Eskdale granite has equal sized small granules, and is the crimson/pink of autumnal elder leaves. The quarry is now closed, but the glittering pink stone faces the walls of Bootle station and can be seen at points along the miniature Eskdale railway. The Bootle walls are termed polygonal random, and faced with red sandstone to good effect. Muncaster School is built of random granite, and at Muncaster Castle the high garden walls are pink granite with the entrance way sporting red sandstone quoins as ornament.

At the other end of the region's curve of granite outcrops lies the more famous pink quarry at Shap, where its two shades are known as Dark Shap and Light Shap. The difference is in the amount of grey and black crystals mixed with the pink feldspar, which also varies in depths of shade. These feldspar crystals shine in their matrix, and though quite large they are not as long as those in Cornish granite, but produce an effect of rounded pink spots. Quarrymen here explained that Shap granite should more correctly be named Feldspar Porphyry. And I was told that the extra brilliance of a tomato coloured piece showed it was about to disintegrate: 'rotten — past its time — wearing out'.

Shap granite has been popular for polishing, and the Victorians particularly appreciated it, so it is found for instance on the Albert Memorial, London. More functionally this granite was used in the construction of Liverpool and Glasgow docks. Now it is used for aggregates and roadstone.

About a mile north, along the A6 road, is the Blue Shap quarry. This seems rather a misnomer, as the walls are a gloomy grey black. This stone is unlike any other granite, the tiny crystals being only just visible, yet there are a few light streaks to relieve the dense dark rock; and for monumental work the blue stone must have been aptly funereal. Here, as in so many other quarries, a great number of stone masons once worked.

The last granite outcrop lies north, in the Threlkeld area east of Keswick. This is also quite different from more familiar granite, and is called 'bastard' locally. It is a very solid compacted stone of greenish, sandy mud colour. The last time this stone was used for building was in 1965. The tower of the Roman Catholic church in Keswick, dedicated to the Lady of the Lakes, was then completed. One stonemason, Harry Page, cut the stone and was rightly pleased with the result. The walls are random and in sunlight the green tinge shows up well.

Cobblestones

These large rounded stones are found in many places throughout the region. They are the obvious result of the last Ice Age, and are smaller editions of the strange erratic boulders seen in numerous places. The cobblestones, ice-worn or water-worn, were originally left by the retreating glaciers and may have travelled long distances. So they do not necessarily belong to the native rock of their landing place, and their colours are as varied as the different rocks they represent. People took them from the rivers or the moraines, or cleared them from their fields, and refer to them as field stones now. They are used whole, or split in half sometimes for houses, but mainly for roadside or field walling. The pattern is frequently made of alternate rows of thin slate, and the rounded stone.

Another type of cobblestone can be found by the west coast. Near Bootle station at least one barn and garage are to be seen, with strong walls of dark slate alternating with grey, brown, black and ink blue cobbles from the sea shore. The same stones are used in the nearby coastal dikes.

4.   The Knoll, near Ambleside — former home of Harriet Martineau and a fine example of 'watershot' masonry. *(Bob Collins)*

5. 'Riving' slate at a quarry near Elterwater. *(W. R. Mitchell)*

QUARRIES

THE quarries in Cumbria vary, of course, according to their different stones and positions. So Kirkstone stands high up in its open fell landscape, to be seen across the valley from the western end of the Kirkstone Pass. The imposing Shap quarries are near the famous summit, so often blocked with snow in a hard winter. On the other hand Tilberthwaite and Honister are in the heart of the mountains, the one surrounded by trees and the other close to the pass, while Threlkeld is in the open above its village, from where we looked down on to the roofs and a present-day quarryman, Bill Ibbotson, could point out the houses of retired masons he advised visiting.

Many quarries are surprisingly old. For instance the great complex at Kirkby-in-Furness, now known as the Burlington Quarries, may have been worked since the late seventeenth century. And the Coniston, Tilberthwaite and Honister quarries are known to have been working since the mid-eighteenth century. Owing to the difficult terrain Honister was one of the hardest from which to transport the stone. Loads had to be sent across a high packhorse route, called Mose's Trod, over the western edge of Great Gable, to be finally off-loaded on to vessels at Ravenglass — a hard fifteen miles for man and beast. This continued until the early eighteen hundreds when roads were improved, and more stone went to local markets.

About one hundred years ago quarrying started in Shap. As one quarryman remarked, 'there are granite outcrops from Shap to Durham, but it's only Shap where it can be got'. By the end of the last century, quarrying was one of the most important industries in the Lake District.

In the earliest days hewing was all done by hand, and no explosives were used before the seventeenth century. The choice then was gunpowder which produced large lumps of rock, suitable to be broken further by hand and dressed on the spot. Nowadays gelignite is used: 'blows it to smithereens, but that's what you need for road stone', as Harry Page of Threlkeld explained.

Some of the fine old quarries have been described as 'now literally industrial monuments to the past'. Today those that are working are so radically changed, through supplying aggregates and roadstone, that only a small number still produce building material. The Cumbria Stone Quarry produces limestone which can be seen on garden walls in Burneside, and New Red Sandstone from Cleator Moor is to be seen in repair work in Carlisle Cathedral.

However, in the slate quarries there is still a big demand for their beautiful coloured stone, the greens in particular, so much appreciated far beyond the Lake District. This is used less for roof tiles, as it used to be, but is found in wall cladding and in 'weathershot' random walling, as well as for ornamental purposes.

There are four kinds of slate classified according to its fineness. The coarsest is 'Peg' and so through to 'Tom' and 'County' to 'London' the top quality. In the old days the 'ryver' — the man using the 'ryver', the splitting hammer — sat side by side with the 'dresser' who cut and shaped the edges, just as such men had done for generations. The riving hammer cut a 'cleg' into a series of smooth slabs, around two and a half inches thick, and from that about eight slates a quarter inch thick were produced.

The general bustle and noise of the quarries in those days must have been tremendous when one considers the numbers of working men employed. In Shap blue quarry Tom Mallinson, now a gate man, described the scene. He worked forty seven years in the same quarry, and forty of those were as a smith. To forty stone masons, with three or four apprentices, there would be two blacksmiths, and one smith apprentice, sharpening and tempering the masons' tools.

In Threlkeld, Harry Page told of thirty to forty sheds with one mason working in each, a larger shed being used if an apprentice worked alongside, as he did with his father.

The dressed stone was removed into a bogey, a 'sled' with four wheels, each containing a ton. Quarry work can only be learnt on the spot, not in a school. 'Those were the days, and those are the skills that are going out', said Bill Ibbotson.

Now the quarries are even more noisy with their huge pieces of machinery. One essential is the crusher which will crush two hundred and fifty tons of rock in a day. Then the differing grades of grits are produced for aggregates and for mortar and cement. However, the same machine, with coarser blades, can produce blocks the right size for the builders.

PATTERNS AND METHODS

RANDOM WALLING is a general description of any wall which is built of rough, hard stone with a minimum amount of working or dressing. Their patterns are possibly like our basic diagrams, but there are many variations beyond those. In the building trade this is known as random rubble walling, as rubble means a hard stone. However, a shortened version is rubble walling, and this is confusing. To most of us rubble denotes damaged masonry, so I will hold to the word random.

An expert, Albert Bowness of Little Langdale, explained, 'In the old pre-war days house walls were solid stone, two feet thick and one ton of stone to every yard. In one day you could only make one yard high and one yard horizontal, if using all cut stone. But it would be two and a half yards if using a mix of cobbles and greenstone for instance.' (Greenstone is the term, in this area, whatever the colour, for any slate off-cuts suitable for building.)

Nowadays the cost of stone is high. Cobblestone is from £5 to £25 per ton and greenstone is £55, and slates vary from £400 to £730 a ton. So the economical method is by facing, where one ton of stone stretches to five yards, according to Bowness. The stone is faced on to an inner wall of concrete blocks; a damp-proof course membrane is the next layer, with varied random stone mortared to it. The process is shown in the illustration (6). One example of a faced wall with mixed stone can be seen on the rounded wall of a house in Troutbeck (7).

To understand the terms for the patterns and methods we begin with the basics. The usual stone-laying method is known in the trade as **Ordinary Coursing,** and a **Random Coursed** stone wall is built in the same way by placing one stone above the joint of the pair below, giving an effect of strict parallel lines (8).

Uncoursed Random no longer keeps to this tidy order, but every stone whatever size is fitted in economically and there is a pleasing, lively broken pattern (9, 10).

Polygonal Style is also shown in the Code of Practice diagrams. It is not seen frequently in Cumbria but can be found in the west of the county at Bootle station made of glittering red granite (11, 12)

Watershot or Weathershot. The 'British Standard Institution Code of Practice Walling: Stone Masonry' describes this method as rough-faced Random Slate, and it is entitled Lake District Masonry. These walls are built in such a way that the sloping set of the stones allows the rain to run off. The deceptive appearance is of a dry wall, as the mortar is invisible. There are many good and attractive examples with different sizes and cuts of green, blue, grey or rust coloured slates for instance in Keswick, Grasmere or Ambleside. (13, 14)

6. Mixed stone facing in process of building at Low Colwith. *(Frank Bodman)*

7. Rounded house wall of mixed stones joined to older slate wall — Troutbeck. *(Janet Bodman)*

Random walling

8. Random coursed walling.

9. Uncoursed random walling.

10. Garden wall of uncoursed random pattern — Burneside. *(Frank Bodman)*

Polygonal style

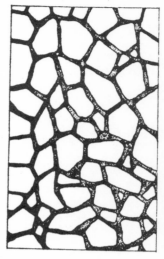

11.   Polygonal style walling.

12.   Polygonal style — Bootle station. *(Frank Bodman)*

Watershot walling

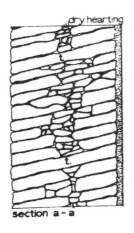

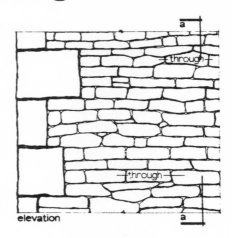

13. **Watershot or weathershot — Lake District masonry.**

14. **Slate in watershot style on house wall at Keswick.** *(Colin Whittle)*

Cobblestone and Slate walls can be seen in various house and garden walls, especially bold in the west, near the turf and cobble dikes shown in *Lakeland Walls*. Our example is in Bootle. **(15)**

Cavity walls are expensive because they are double-sided. They are common as garden walls, often tapered slightly for drainage, and they will show various toppings.

Bedding

The wall must be made virtually indestructible, so the Code of Practice states: 'The strength of a rubble wall depends on the skill of the mason in selecting, laying and bonding the stones.' These can be laid with the edge facing outwards, 'edge-bedded', which required the stone's bed in the wall to be horizontal, as it was in the natural bedding plane in the quarry. If it is laid with its bed standing upright it is 'face-bedded' which is considered bad practice by the experts, as it erodes faster. Granite is the exception to this rule because its elements are so compressed.

The choice of stone

There are few independent small quarries left now, so generally the stone is brought from the different quarries owned by the Burlington group. One exception is Wetherlam, High Fell, which is worked by just three men, producing whitish greenstone.

To save transport costs there was a long tradition of using material as near the site as possible. Fortunately sometimes stone can be 'won', as they say, from the site itself. Old used stone can be re-used but then care must be taken to remove all trace of old mortar. This has been practised for centuries when material was filched from ruined monasteries or castles, and now stone is recycled from old barns or other derelict buildings.

Pattern making

It is not easy to discover how exactly the pattern is arrived at. One waller claims, 'You know it in your head', and it seems that he holds a pattern in his mind's eye, and in his hands. They all agree, 'You must never put a stone back once you have picked it up. Time is money.' There can be no hesitation or second thoughts.

The quoins or corner stones give the firm outline, and the various sized stones all fit into each man's scheme. One rule is that where large stones, 'jumpers', are used in a face-bedded wall they must not touch.

In polygonal work the stones are cut almost to uniform size, and the pattern looks like a crazy pavement up-ended. With watershot there is no particular design, but there is very skilled repetitive laying. In all these examples no wall is built with ordinary coursing.

Pointing

This is infrequently used here, in contrast to the south-west of England. One example of ridged or 'snail creep' pointing can be found in the east of the county, and flush pointing is shown in polygonal work in the western side. In

15.   Garden wall of cobblestone and slate — Bootle. *(Janet Bodman)*

the heart of the Lake District, as we have already found, the mortar is invisible in watershot masonry and in most random walling of mixed stone. In the illustration the mortar is 'laid back' and can hardly be seen **(13, 14)**. It is rare to see any mortar misused by heavy handling or smearing, demonstrating that the Cumbrian mason generally has great respect for his material.

Mortar

In general use this is in the proportion of four to one sand/cement, mixed with a plasticiser. Builder's sand used to come from Windermere, but now it comes from Penrith. At one time clay was used for bedding, as sand and lime were not readily available. This had to be kept well back from the face to prevent the rain washing it out. Although mortar is now used the custom continues, while the original reason for the practice is forgotten.

Dry Walling

In considering patterns and methods we should look briefly at dry walling. These walls are such a feature of the landscape in the Lake District, and have been since the eighteenth century. They are not only used as boundary walls but provide much needed shelter for the sheep. One pattern characteristic is their 'outgangs' of two walls narrowing, like a funnel, to draw the sheep off the fells down into their pens in the valley. And their sheep or 'hogg' holes are similar to those in the Cornish stone 'hedges' — square holes, allowing the sheep to move through from one pasture to another without hindrance. Topping styles can vary, and one attractive method is where a single row of larger squared slates or 'cams' is sloped at an angle.

A good new wall of mixed stones can be found by the roadside at Dunmail Raise. The characteristic 'through' stones of the north can be seen jutting through on both sides of a few field walls, but appear less frequently here than in the Pennines and areas east of Cumbria.

THE MASONS, THEIR TOOLS AND CRAFT

THERE were no architects in the Middle Ages, and so the craftsmen were both designers and builders. Highly skilled men, they would travel from one project to another, being employed by the great royal or monastic houses of the day. These travelling specialists — freemasons — went far and wide with their small number of tools, and a pattern book, to produce grandly imposing castles or beautiful abbeys and cathedrals, of which so many still stand today. Other stone workers, from the district, would be drawn in to help in these large enterprises.

The lesser skilled men were the diggers, layers, paviers and wallers, working within the rules of their guilds, and paid precise wages for their specific functions. They were unsung and unnamed, nevertheless they could also construct more modest buildings in their own right. These are the farms, cottages, barns and bridges we are studying, and some are small miracles in their way; many are still standing after centuries of wear and weather, robust and sturdy as their builders.

The waller's job was often a solitary one. He might work away out in the country, with no design, and very little equipment other than his simple bag of tools. It is hard for those of us who have never attempted it to understand how it was tackled. Two writers have endeavoured to explain these special abilities. Dorothy Hartley *(Made in England)* states, 'I believe much of the old rockman's calculations, even now, is of the same curious method as the old shepherd's counting; not a mental appreciation of separate numbers, but a mass appreciation. Perhaps this thinking in block and weight simplified the rockman's vision, for study of many small buildings will show the most complicated difficulties tackled and solved by his steady structural skill without line or figure on paper.'

This is an example of the oral tradition of teaching — the older generation passing on their skills by words, and demonstrating by hand to the younger men and boys. There is nothing written, but a quick sketch drawn in the earth will suffice, as I discovered when some wallers clarified a method to me in this way.

Ewart-Evans in *Days That We Have Seen* says, 'The knowledge is in his bones you could say, an insight, an intuition and none the less valuable for that', and today he claims 'the hand-tool character of work' in country communities shows that 'the consciousness of the older inhabitants is still firmly fixed in a way of life centuries before the modern changes. Through these older people the umbilical time-cord still remains uncut'. So tradition continues as if through a relay race, but the stick handed on is a live link, a growing sequence which few of us experience. But if you find a skilled craftsman he will be well worth listening to, and he will enjoy talking about his work, and his stone and sometimes of his training.

Apprenticeships have developed from the old guild standards. There are a variety of schemes throughout England, linked with the technical colleges. Some are run by local councils, some by small firms and some by major contractors, whose walls can be seen beside the motorways.

As one waller said, 'We went straight from school at fourteen and got our indentures at twenty-one. In the old days there would have been five builders' apprentices to every journeyman. He might have been through an apprenticeship or he might have been one of the best quarrymen brought into the trade.' Journeymen masons were until fairly recently those who travelled widely for their work. In the past this was encouraged for them to gain experience, after their seven year apprenticeship, and to make way for new men to take their place. The general ratio at present is usually one apprentice to five or six masons — the reverse of previous times.

Albert Bowness, speaking of Cumbria in 1978, said, 'There is now about one trained man to each building firm.' He incidentally had two besides himself and his son, and to these four was one apprentice, and stonework represented 10 per cent of all their contracts. His son Richard has trained three apprentices in the last six years, working alongside four trained wallers. He finds the present ruling of three years far too short and hopes it will be extended again to four, or better still five years, now there are more youngsters willing and available.

There were masons in the quarries, as traditionally stones were 'hammer-dressed' or 'knocked and chopped' there for building material. Now the walling mason does this on site, and even reused stone needs some shaping. Harry Page, a long-retired quarry mason, explained, 'We served seven years, but a witty lad could learn faster than that. Barring two wars I worked all my life in Threlkeld quarry dressing stone. I came out of my time before 1914 and made pavement setts.' After tarred pavements were introduced his skills were turned to dressing stone for building, 'Always varied work and interesting right up to my retirement.' He shows as if there were a stone in his hand, 'You had to find the RID in the stone and cut *there*.'

His accuracy and skill were much admired by a younger man, Bill Ibbotson, still working in Threlkeld Quarry, 'These masons had real skill, they could tap a stone with a hammer and it would break exactly where they wanted. But with any of us, with this granite, it would go all ways.'

Tools

Many of the mason's tools are the same as the quarryman's and have changed very little over the centuries. Quarry tools used by the Romans were identical (as elaborate stone-carvers' tools for freestone are replicas of those from Ancient Egypt). The stone mallet, sledge hammer, cold chisel and various picks are those most often used. For mortar work the trowel and hand-hod, or mortar-board, are specific to the mason. The Cumbrian quarryman's name for hammer is 'tifler' and a mallet is a 'maul'. A waller used a two pound walling hammer with a double head, one end a square of 1½ inches for hammering, and the other a 1½ inch chisel edge. A cutting chisel has a two inch head and cuts across the grain, whereas a riving chisel 'cuts down the bed of the stone'. A 'punch' is a small cold chisel with a half inch head used for 'plucking' quoins.

The tools used for slate are much finer, as seen in the slater's pick and claw. As Hartley explains, 'to handle slate is a matter of knack and skill, rather than strength, and the facility for the finest work is not easily acquired. Some old workmen develop a wonderful sense of touch and balance, and will split slate true to a hair, with a very light blow exactly placed.'

The modern tools are now tipped with tungsten, whereas in the thirties 'you had to have a good smith to keep sharpening and tempering your tools for you', as an expert smith claims. He reckons the correct tempering 'is done by touch and eye as much as by the heat.'

There is a strong bond between a craftsman and his tools, as we all know in a minor way when using our garden or kitchen utensils. The more a tool is used the more it is the extension of hand and arm, and the handle is polished with repeated pressure, and handling and the palm's sweat. It can also become a tiresome adversary on which to vent ill-will, when frustration sets in. But usually tools are handled with care, and each is treated as a friend. Long after retirement the craftsman keeps them and speaks of them with pride, and perhaps tells of the hard struggle in their original purchase in the early days of his apprenticeship, which meant saving shilling by shilling, week by week.

The stone worker's craft

There is an unfounded rumour circulating which unfortunately calls this a dying craft. To counter this we have the expert opinion of Arch Ireson, the experienced and well known stonemasonry consultant and sculptor: 'It may possibly be true in one district, or in one person's experience, it is simply NOT so nationally. Looking back over the last sixty years or so, the scene has of course changed, and there are not so many masons as there were. Since labour costs have increased and more machinery has been introduced, it is no longer possible for the very small firm to keep full-time wallers or maintain expensive machinery. The stone craftsmen have tended to go to larger firms and into towns, and now another generation of good young craftsmen are succeeding.' The single-handed or full-time waller is fairly rare; he is more likely to be the expert in a builder's firm where say a third of his time will be spent on stone walling.

The only way of expanding the stone waller's craft is through the practical support of architects, planners, councillors, employers and conservationists. Fortunately there is now a gradual increase in those who appreciate stone. As one quarry manager stated, 'People have become weary with synthetic things, and they long for natural materials.' This may be too sweeping a generalisation, but it seems to be fair comment on the Cumbrian scene.

One very positive note sounds when learning about The Men of the Stones. This is a society which advocates, very actively, the use of local stone and other natural materials, and encourages and supports training centres. Their secretary, Arch Ireson, offers wise advice: 'We still believe that the best possible training a young willing mason can have is with his father, or a good small firm in his own locality, and on the native materials of his district.'

The Dartington Vernacular Exhibition of 1975 asked that 'we may acquire a new respect for builders and craftsmen who shaped the environment'. We need more exhibitions of that kind, to increase our awareness, but in Cumbria there are lively reminders in walls throughout the region. To encourage an appreciation of the landscape, and its various features, the Lake District National Park Board has provided special centres with permanent exhibitions. At Brockhole near Windermere there is a walling instruction area for the do-it-yourself enthusiast. But this is only concerned with dry-walling.

Vernacular building in the Lakes has the traditional down-to-earth principle of building to last, whilst also insisting on good proportions. There are no pretensions now, as in Victorian days, and no irrelevant embellishments. The results are very pleasing and have become an integral part of the landscape. The region is fortunate in having the Lake District Planning Board whose brief is to 'ensure that new building is of the kind which will not offend the eye of the majority of this and following generations'. Surely well beyond this ruling many of the modern stone buildings are a positive delight to the eye, and so long as the traditional craftsmen's skills are consistently encouraged the prospects are hopeful.

Further Reading

The Pattern of English Building, Alec Clifton-Taylor. Faber 1972.
Illustrated Handbook of Vernacular Architecture, R. W. Brunskill. Faber 1970.
Your House: the Outside View, John Prizeman. Hutchinson 1975.
Stone in Building, John Ashurst & Francis G. Dimes. Architectural Press 1977.
A History of Building Materials, Norman Davey. Phoenix House 1961.